Camouflaged

Paranoia™

Camouflaged

Paranoia™

A Path in the Right Direction

Chief Roy A Millmore
Law Enforcement Instructor

To all those souls who have perished at the hands of evil and all those who have become victims and those ignored by people who failed to do the right thing.

Author's note

We cannot people-proof everything or anything. We can only take the information we have and follow a path in the right direction. I would urge the reader not to make the mistake of believing it is totally dangerous to assist their fellow man. In contrast it would be wrong to accept daily routine as totally safe. The purpose of this writing is to point out the necessity to engage your thought process to maintain the safety and security for yourself and those you love. Do the right thing, but do it with contemplation before you act. Do it under a standard of camouflaged–paranoia.

Camouflaged-paranoia™ is a term I coined more than thirty years ago as a young police officer in the mid to late 1970's. I had been trained via the military in 1969 to be alert to anyone and anything that might bring harm to me or my fellow soldiers, in the jungles of Vietnam.

Serving in the U.S. Army; I had been deployed with the 105 Howitzer Group; 6th 29th Artillery Bravo Company as an artillery gunner, attached to the 3rd of the 12th, 4th Infantry in the central highlands. Only months in country; I was transferred from the Air Mobile 105 Howitzers to be the forward observer with Alpha Company 3rd of the 12th.

There we roamed the central highlands with orders to locate and destroy any and all enemy caches, Viet Cong gorilla fighters or North Vietnamese Regular Soldiers.

One hilltop after another and one valley into another, we fought; firefight after firefight until we finished our tour and were sent home.

Many of my fellow soldiers unfortunately went home in a box and others with severe injuries, both physical and psychological. Returning to the states, now honorably discharged; I felt there was more to be done. Not in the battlefields of heavy vegetation and jungles of Vietnam but on the battlefields of our city streets. Only months after taking off the green uniform identifying me as a soldier and a Vietnam Veteran, I put on a new uniform, this time a blue one.

I was now a soldier in the civilian world of not just fighting for this country's freedom but ensuring our government upheld the rights of individuals. This was empowering to my self esteem and I have been proud of serving in these capacities without ever looking back.

There is however a common integrate part of both my being a U.S. soldier and a civilian police officer.

This portion of what makes each career intertwine successfully and constructively is training.

Training is a subject that with forty years of service, has afforded me the opportunity to establish an expertise. Being a soldier in Vietnam began the first introduction into camouflaged-paranoia. It was not so camouflaged during the time in Vietnam; it was far more open and petulant.

I think before we go any further into the history of this term we need to understand, these words can only be adequately used together. That is as two words not one. They cannot be separated or we chance the perception and distort the intended meaning.

So looking at the words independently first, will help us understand how and why both words must be used together to meet the standard of meaning and usage.

The following is the "Webster's New World Dictionary" definitions of these terms.

camouflaged; "A disguise; deception; to disguise (a thing or person) for concealment."

paranoia; Para- beside + nous, the mind, 'a mental disorder characterized by delusions, as of grandeur or, esp., persecution, Paranoid.'

"camouflaged-paranoia™" my term, my definition;

> 1. "To disguise one's thoughts of suspicious intention or action on the part of another." 2. "To be vigilant of other people's intentions or actions."

Now obviously the first term "camouflaged" is used in its blatant meaning herein; to disguise. The term "paranoia" is used in its common meaning among lay persons to be; suspicious, fearful or mistrustful. I do not use this term in a sense of grandeur or paucity.

When I use and teach this term, I mean it in the sense that every person(s), especially police officers and soldiers; must always have their minds tuned in and turned on. They must be aware and in fact alert without prejudice, to the very real possibility that anyone can harm them.

What do I mean without prejudice? I mean that it does not matter how old, how young or any other distinguishing identifiers there are; that person can harm you.

There have been children as young as nine whom with intent, shot and killed police officers and there have been women as old as eighty who have shot and killed police officers.

There have been well dressed people and sloppy hobos who have shot and killed police officers and there are housewives who have stabbed police officers for helping them when their husbands had just beaten the wife.

The above are extreme examples, but very real and happen with far too much regularity. On one of the most routine duties as a police officer like millions of my colleagues, I have been shoved, spit on, and yelled at.

On numerous occasions over the years, there have been attempts to take my weapon. They have tried to take the weapon from my holster which I wore or the shotgun/rifle in my police unit.

But there is a far more serious problem in our world with the general public. We address these problems in part, when we teach our children continuously; "DO NOT TALK TO STRANGERS!"

Herein is a prime example which becomes evident. We must all have and teach the cautious mindset of "camouflaged-paranoia". This is not an innate human trait. It is not the sixth sense or woman's intuition people refer to and it is not the police officer or soldier's "gut feeling".

Without this referenced state of mind taught and practiced, each of us allows ourselves to be in harms way. When we are taught to be a police officer or a soldier, this mindset becomes standard as it does in the teaching of martial arts.

Obviously I am not advocating everyone walk around believing those near them are "out to get them". Nor do I mean you should stay home and hide in the closet. This is generally the perception from an individual who call themselves a Doctor of Psychiatry. Unfortunately, I have found most of these individuals cannot see past the whack jobs on the couch, with the mental disorders that are in desperate need of medical treatment.

The "doctor" often has little to no experience with exposure to the real world on the streets as it pertains to human reaction on the spot. They only refer to the books from the prestigious schools they attended. This took them from their more often than not; "Leave it to Beaver" home settings.

Having said this, let me also give appropriate kudos to those doctors who have learned to listen in full context of what is being said and implied. Those doctors have had real life exposure and understand that parsing words will distort the meaning of statements and terms. The doctors, who have an open mind outside the books, often have a PHD in Psychology versus a Psychiatrist MD.

So why do I use this strong word of camouflaged in front of paranoia? Because there is seldom reason to "jump the gun".

You should not allow your inner thoughts of "what does this person want?' or 'what is this person up to?" to be exposed. Until there is an act on their part to provide strength to your thought of the possibility that you will be harmed.

But you should always have the possibility in your mindset. It can save you troubles and maybe even your life.

Let me give you an example that has happened everywhere in the world.

A kind and good hearted person observes a stranger or even a known associate, broken down on the side of the road. Or maybe simply dropped their grocery bag in the parking lot of the store and you want to help.

You stop and ask; "Are you okay? Do you need help?" The other person says "Well I thought I was okay, but then this car of mine broke down and won't start." Or the other person, "This grocery bag ripped apart." This is followed by, "If you could give me a ride" or "help me pick up these items in the parking lot, I would appreciate your help."

You say; "Jump in, where can I take you?" Or in the other case, you get out of your vehicle and bend down to help pick up the groceries. The next thing you know there is a gun or a knife in your side and you are on your way for a one way ride. Possibly the last one you will ever take.

Wow, that is paranoid! Yes it is. But how about instead of being a good hearted person, you also become vigilant with a twist. The twist being you should be very careful and help the person by calling someone on the phone; like the police for the person stranded on the side of the road.

Or make sure others in the parking lot know you are helping someone and scream when necessary. Don't turn your back to them when bent over and do not bend to put anything into their vehicle. Hand the groceries to them and stand upright. Be ready if you have to run, if that's all you can do. But there is no need to show or expose that you are suspicious and cause a problem that did not exist in the first place. That is the camouflaged portion of this statement.

Most of the time there will be nothing wrong and the person you want to help is only a person in need of help. I understand this, but becoming complacent to possible danger is exactly what causes people to become a victim.

In police work and of course as a soldier; complacency gets you harmed and often times killed. It also puts the general public, the nice person into harms way.

I already gave you two examples for common folks that can become problematic and three if you count the common knowledge of what we tell our children.

As a soldier, letting one's guard down, becoming complacent will get your limbs blown off and/or a bullet in your body; the one way ticket. As a soldier, there is one saving grace and that is the soldier does not have to hide their paranoia as often. They're on deployment in a war zone and their reaction, although calculated based on training and justified, is often with aggression.

In addition to the injury and death scenarios for soldiers in a war zone, the same is true for police officers. However, the rules of engagement are very different.

There are far more outcomes in police work. Mostly because an officer must make every attempt to hide or camouflage their paranoia, or the incident can expand into real problematic issues.

These issues can manifest into career damaging, political fallout for the officer and their department and or injury to the public. Violations of the constitution can be misread or even confirmed and tremendous financial burdens placed onto the officer, their families and their hiring authorities. But at no time should an officer become complacent. The risks are simply too high. They are too high for the general public as well.

So I have taken it upon myself to teach and explain this concept to everyone who will listen and the feedback has been inspiring. Several people have returned; sometimes years after hearing my explanation and examples, to report that "camouflaged-paranoia" has helped them feel safer and they still live normal everyday lives, unafraid to assist others when necessary.

Unfortunately there are those who have a mindset far too liberal for their own safety. They state that it is not normal to be suspicious of every person. They say "not everyone is out to hurt you or do you harm". I say that I agree with them in the general context of what they believe.

The problem here is; these very fine, well meaning individuals with a liberal mindset do not have the experience to qualify their statements. Interesting enough however, is when they become the victim, their mindset changes. I should say most of the time they change but sadly, not always.

Everyone can become complacent even warriors and police officers. It was several years after I had been discharged from the military and graduated from the police academy. I had been taught and in fact, had it drilled into my head; "Never become complacent." "Always be on your guard."

Then one very cold and foggy night while on patrol, I observed a vehicle parked along the side of the road. It was not very busy and there were only a few officers on duty. I saw no need to call for back up. I did advise the dispatcher where I was and that I would be checking out the vehicle.

At first I thought it was abandoned but as I approached I could see a female sitting in the driver seat. She was alone and crying her eyes out.

I walked up to the driver window and she was very polite. She was a middle aged lady who was dressed in her night gown. We spoke for a while and finally, she told me her trouble. She began telling me that her husband, a police officer for another city, had been having an affair and they had a hurtful boisterous verbal fight.

She was teary eyed and her voice shook the entire time we spoke, obviously distraught. I offered to call another relative but she refused, noting the incident was already too embarrassing. I asked if she had someplace to go and she advised she would return home after giving her husband time to leave the house.

Do you have children I asked? She replied that they did but there was an older son at home and he would take care of the two little ones until she returned.

By this time I had become complacent and stooped at the driver's door to speak with her eye to eye. I felt I might be intimidating her standing above her and looking down as I stood there. I was trying to comfort her and find a way to get her home without upsetting her any further.

Finally it hit me. I had indeed become complacent and suddenly the hair stood up on the back of my neck. I asked cautiously if she had any weapons and she said yes. My heart began beating so loud I thought she could hear it echoing in the fog.

I slowly rested my hand as naturally as possible onto my weapon. I stood slowly without causing her to notice I was doing anything but rearranging my position. Then she raised her hand from her left side and said "I guess you want this". She was holding a six inch 357 magnum, fully loaded.

Thank God, I thought as my heart settled down; that she did not point that weapon at me. She could have easily killed me or I her at that very moment. The tension was almost palpable and she took notice. I had her safely hand me the weapon.

She said, "I am sorry, I should have put this down and told you I had it when you first walked up." I thought to myself that would have been nice. But at the same time it was my complacency that would have been to blame, if anything tragic had occurred.

I think that was the very night when I coined this term, "camouflaged-paranoia". I have told this story many times in an attempt to prove that anyone can become complacent in very dangerous situations.

I say please believe me that when you pick up a hitchhiker, a friend of the family or assist someone, particularly a stranger; that it can and often does turn tragic.

How often do we hear people say, "I did not think that person could do such a thing?" "This type of stuff just does not happen in this town or neighborhood or wherever."

"My God, I can't believe this happened." "We don't lock our doors here because there has never been a reason to do so. We always have trusted each other."

I know it appears that I am building a case to live in fear. This is not my intention and I do not believe we should. I do without question, believe we must stay aware and we must be vigilant. We should understand that everyone is capable of perpetrating a wrong and everyone is a potential victim.

We will spend hours hopefully teaching our children to not speak to strangers. Then we turn right around and walk alone into a dark parking lot or down a lonely beach at night and some of us are never seen again.

We leave our doors unlocked, convinced the neighborhood is safe. But give no thought to the chump who wanders in from another city, down the street or right next door.

Everyone likes to think they are smart and many believe they will react powerfully and strong if they ever need to do so. They fool themselves into complacency simply because they do not practice staying alert. They do not practice challenging someone who should be challenged. They do not speak up and advise others of concerns, believing they will be looked upon as crazy or paranoid.

Recently a car salesman told my wife and me a story.

"I am over six foot tall and in pretty good shape. I have a loud voice and always thought I could take an aggressive stand if necessary. Then one night there was a guy in my yard, he obviously did not belong there and it frightened me. I pointed at him and started to say something. As I recall it would have been; what are you doing in my yard? But what came out was soft and merely inaudible. In fact it was a stammering whisper. Thank God only my presence caused him to run away. There is no doubt my believing I could convince someone I was a tough guy, flew out the window."

Just like measuring up a small innocent looking Joe Blow, thinking he is a pushover can get you're butt kicked; it can just as easily cause you to become a victim. In other words don't let someone's appearance fool you, or don't judge the book by its cover.

Have you ever hired a contractor to work on the outside of your home? Then found you had to leave the house to run an errand or two? Well I have and I knew and trusted the contractor. When I realized I forgot my wallet, I returned immediately.

When I drove up the driveway I could hear our son's drums being played inside the house and no one was working outside. The workers took it upon themselves to enter our home and help themselves to playing the drums.

And who knows what else they would have done if I had not returned so quickly. This may be a mild example, but it stands that if I would have given the matter any thought, I would not have left the house unattended.

It is further interesting to me that my wife, like other police officer's wives, is often ridiculed by friends for outward concern. I can recall the wife of my partner long ago, when she refused to allow her friend to pick up a hitchhiker. The story was if you pick up this person even if you know who he is from the grocery store, drop me off. I will call my husband to come get me.

My wife has often told stories where her friends speak of common daily events such as going to recycle. My wife asks, "Did you remove your address and name from the boxes before you tossed them into the recycling bin?" The reply is, "That is just like a cop's wife."

My wife then will make an attempt to explain. This is how criminals know who has the new big screen televisions or computers. They also make an attempt at finding out who is in the home and when. They do not always wait until the house is empty, if you get the drift.

Having explained the darker side of camouflaged–paranoia, wherein the extreme may occur to you without practicing the thought pattern. I would be disingenuous if I did not address being on the recipient side of these thoughts, should they be stripped of their camouflage.

There are a multitude of cause and effects which will occur and they in turn can also be devastating to the innocent. In my dedication to law enforcement and with skills in observing and listening, my practiced camouflaged-paranoia must be balanced.

I would caution everyone to do the same by first acknowledging each person is an individual and reacts differently to similar situations that others have experienced. This I think is where we get into a quandary.

I have interviewed many people from all walks of life in all sorts of incidents, which give rise to the full spectrum of emotions. I have delivered enough death notices; have had direct contact with the death of friends on the battlefield and in civilian life with family members; to know everyone expresses their emotions differently.

Some people let the flood gates open and others are subdued, processing their grief and other emotions within. Often the subdued person comes across as emotionless and icy at best. This is the example that makes my point.

Because most people fall somewhere in the middle of the emotional spectrum, we are left with a thought of; that person shows no emotion, so they must be guilty.

This of course is considered in law enforcement but it falls below the scale of balance because it is a wavering factor.

If an investigator places too much emphasis on a person of interest's emotions, they may very well turn the wrong corner. This is when character and emotion begin to trump intent, motive and opportunity.

You can see the problem as it becomes obvious. The detective with good intention leads the investigation and the trial into a not guilty verdict or an innocent person could be convicted.

The same is true without any criminal involvement when we strip our practiced paranoia of its camouflage. We tend to bring harm to those we suspect of having nefarious ideas. When indeed that person is only slightly different from what we think is normal.

Not only does the display or lack of emotion play a part in our perception, so too does a visual observation. I mentioned previously, that many people have a preconceived visual of a criminal.

A potential witness in a neighborhood often describes anyone who fits their preconceived visual and overlooks the well-dressed well-mannered neighbor; who was in fact standing on the corner at an odd hour.

Why do we think investigators hand people their business card and say, "If you think of anything else call me." or the detective returns to re-interview everyone in the case files?

I have re-interviewed witnesses and potential witnesses two, three, four and even five times; especially in priority cases. I know it seems like we don't know what we are doing or that we are wasting time.

Often people inherently did not think a piece of information or a particular person was relevant. But to the detective it might mean breaking the case and even saving a life.

It sounds almost counter productive when we try to affix logic to the term and the practice of camouflaged-paranoia. But like everything within the human mind, not much is actually cemented in a stone hard brain.

About the only thing we can be sure of is that there are emotions. We just don't know how those emotions play out within each individually. We do not know what, if any, actions or reactions will manifest by the use of those emotions.

If we accept this theory then the question is; when do we appropriately strip our camouflaged-paranoia and tell someone. This hopefully is obvious but in case it might not be, I think a basic guideline would prove beneficial.

Readdressing the issue examples previously stated, let's take them one by one. In the case where someone is broken down on the side of the road and you may or may not know that person.

They tell you their vehicle won't start and may even pretend to avoid putting you out of your way when you ask if you can help.

There is no need to call the police and say, "A person just tried to get me to help him on the side of the road and I think he was creepy." There is a reason to call the police and say, "There is a person broken down on the side of the road who needs help." If they truly were creepy, then tell the police and they will ask additional questions of you.

By calling the police, you stay out of potential harms way and the person gets the help they need. Or if you know that person and really believe they are "a-ok"; at the very least call your family members before you help, to advise who you're helping and why.

Don't forget to tell them where you are, where you are going, and what the vehicle is that is broken down. Do not help until you have done this or you may pay the consequences.

I know this sounds horrible. I know you think you can trust your neighbors and your odd uncle, but you should never throw caution to the wind. When a person goes missing, where does law enforcement look first?

They search your house. You might think they are merely searching for the possibility that the child is hiding in the closet. That is true and they are very hopeful, but they are also mindful that there may be evidence that you or your odd uncle is a person of interest in a potential criminal abduction.

Then they go and search every other potential household of the family and friends and begin to look at teachers, preachers, and playgrounds.

The investigation expands outward not inward. Why? Because the statistics often prove that the perpetrators of nefarious events are close to the family. Now having said this to make my point; I believe experienced detectives do both. They expand outward and inward simultaneously.

In the case where a stranger request your help picking up groceries after their bag ripped open in the parking lot of the grocery store. There is no need to yell rape or cry for help. There is only the need to tell others or ask others around you to assist as well. At the very least, let someone close by know you will be helping a stranger. This can be done easy enough, just say it. "I don't know this person but can you help me pick up their groceries." Just enter into general conversation with someone other than the person you're helping.

If there is no one nearby, go back into the store and ask for additional help or get on your phone and tell someone what you're doing. A mobile phone call is easy to do while you're helping. In any case do not turn your back to the person you're helping and do not put anything into their vehicle. Hand the groceries to them and let them load the vehicle.

Do you allow your child to wander in a store? Any store, the grocery or the mall?

That is a mistake and if this does not bring home the practice of camouflaged-paranoia, I don't know what does. When they are small, tether them to you and when they are teens; don't be their friend, be their parent.

Engage with your children; don't live separate and complete lives. There is a balance and they can have their privacy and their own entertainment. Just monitor the activities closely without alienating the child. In other words; there is no need to hide your concern, just educate your child. There are a multitude of books on this subject if you need them.

I suggest you learn the meaning of their text messages, abbreviations etcetera. Follow their tweets and their facebook and emails.

There are other cautions we should take and think about when it comes to our children. One thing that several parents do is write their child's name in plain sight on their backpacks, on books and on their clothing; like shoes and jackets.

This gives up the child's name to a potential predator. Use a number so the child can identify their property. If a stranger talks to them regarding their parents, have your children ask for a code word that only you and the child knows. If the person does not give the right code word, have your child run.

We have examined the real difficult areas that generate the practice for camouflaged–paranoia. But what about the extended concerns alluded to where a police officer's wife or others talk about throwing the trash out. How about giving the merchant, any merchant your identifying numbers.

Let's address these issues. Criminals in all communities across the USA dig in the trash. Why? So they can find your identifying numbers. Social security, driver's license, credit cards and account numbers. They retrieve your phone bills and monitor the numbers called, what numbers call you.

Then they will call those same numbers to figure out if they can scam the person on the other end or you.

They will sell your driver's license, social security and account numbers. They will use any and all the numbers to their financial gain and your financial ruin.

They will look at the empty packages to determine if your home is worth the time and trouble to burglarize, i.e. the big screen televisions, computers, popular toys or the new limited edition sneakers. So what do you do? Tear off the labels to hide your name, address and the company and product received from your empty packages before disposing.

Shred the identifying numbers and all phone bills, account numbers old and new. Let nothing go into the trash that someone else can use to their advantage. Shredders are cheap today in just about any large retailer.

Now what about those pesky retailers who want as much information as you are willing to part with?

This is tough, because we like receiving emails to tell us when there is a great sale. But often the retailers will sell your phone number and email to other companies.

But that is not my real concern; it is the store employee who requests the information that bothers me. Employee's who jot your information down when you walk away, for their own use.

They are selling or using this information without going through your trash. They don't have to go "dumpster diving". You just handed them all they need, right into their hands, legally. And you will often find it difficult and very expensive to prove you're innocent, when you receive a bill for purchases you did not make. This is especially true when it can be proven that you were at the store, on the day in question.

I would use only one credit card and I recommend you change that card number at least every six months to a year.

I would also be sure to have a red flag on your card for the retailers to check photo identification and signature when the card is used.

When a retailer requests my phone number, I politely refuse and the same thing goes for my email. On the topic of emails; don't open anything you have not requested. I do not open any forwards unless I have direct conversation with the person who sent them to me. Even then it must be of interest to me, or it's a no go.

I know this next hint or suggestion is time consuming but it still prevents fraud and theft. Every time we send an email to others, we immediately remove them from our contacts.

Hacking is big business. It is far more than just your information they get, it is also the others you contact. This also helps deter unwanted emails and most will enter your spam, which you can eliminate all at once without opening.

When it comes to our computers, we should address the wireless connection. I like this feature no doubt. But hackers can sit down the block or next door and connect. After a technician installs a new computer or repairs a problem, change your passwords immediately. For that matter do the same for the good old messy wired connection. It is not always the technician who hacks you.

Hackers are some of the best fraudsters to come along in a hundred years. They still commit the same type of basic crimes, but they can do it without ever making contact with you. They can do it completely unanimously and misdirect their location with the mere click of a button. All they need to know is which buttons and when in what program or which binary codes to use.

This once was a marvel to those of us who had no concept of how a computer works. Today, particularly among our older senior citizens, grandma and grandpa; I hear how smart their child is when it comes to the computers use. They are absolutely right! It has become so easy to manipulate our computers, even a young child who knows nothing else, can become a fraudster.

One of the real hard to swallow statistics is; those grandchildren are often in their teens or early twenties, ripping off grandma and grandpa.

Well you ask, are you crazy or isn't there anyone you trust? My answer is a resounding "no" to the first part. I am simply aware and cautious, practicing camouflaged–paranoia. And an absolute "yes" to the second part. Like everyone else, I trust my immediate family implicitly.

I also trust most of my friends and some of my acquaintances. However, as we get further away from these persons my camouflaged-paranoia engages quickly.

In conclusion of my coined and practiced term, I thought it might be interesting for you to examine your own camouflaged-paranoia now that you have read its meaning and application. To follow, you will find a quiz to test your awareness.

Remember this is not your intuition and it is not your sixth sense or even your gut feeling. It is a conscience thought process which you practice as defined;

1.   "To disguise one's thought of suspicious intention or action on the part of another."

2.   "To be vigilant of other people's intentions or actions."

This practice in one equation is; "Your personal safety and security depends on you."

Quiz:

1. Are you a trusting person who gives everyone and anyone the benefit of the doubt?

2. Do you help people that you do not know, no matter where or when you have been asked?

3. Do you copy the license plate down of vehicles that turn into your driveway when all they do is ask for directions?

4. Do you allow your children to wander in the stores?

5. Do you just stand by and never help anyone who needs help, perhaps they have fallen in the parking lot?

6. Do you throw out your trash without shredding important numbers?

7. Do you ever remove or black out the labels on your cardboard boxes received, before putting them in the trash or recycle bins?

8. Have you ever picked up a hitchhiker that you did not know? If so did you call and tell anyone that you picked up the hitchhiker?

9. Do you willingly give your phone number and or email to the retailers?

10. Do you change your passwords after a technician installs a new computer and or repairs a problem with your old computer?

11. Do you move into a new home, whether you had it built or just purchased or rented it, without changing the locks?

12. Do you change your credit card numbers at least once a year?

13. Do you open emails without knowing exactly who sent them?

14. Do you know that most search engines used maintain a read out of every search you conduct on the internet?

15. Did you know that your provider can remotely use your computer?

16. Do you leave your doors unlocked, or your garage door open at night?

17. Have you stood on the side of the road and waited for help,

then observed the patrol vehicle just drive by? Did you call the police and complain?

18. Do you have a sign in your vehicle that reads; "Call the Police", that you can display if needed?

19. Do your children walk around with their names written in plain view on their clothing?

20. Do you and your children practice passwords to indicate who they're talking with, have your permission for them to respond? Do you tell your children to run for help if the password is not used?

The news has shown that many people will walk past someone in need of assistance, without even a glance in their direction. Is this camouflaged-paranoia? No. This is the new human trait of not caring about anyone but themselves.

If it was camouflaged-paranoia, they would at least call someone else to assist. But no, they just go about their business as if the old person lying in the street is part of the scenery.

Do you think it is okay to assist someone in need of help? I hope you do. Just be very careful and be sure to engage your newly acquired "camouflaged-paranoia."

William Shakespeare wrote:

"Love all, trust a few, do wrong to none."